Conten

CW01635265

Introduction

This is not a booklet to be read once and then discarded. It is a pocket course designed to be used continuously as a fast and easy reference. It is a brief operating manual of professional salesmanship.

The material is hyper-condensed, all padding and unnecessary information has been stripped out. The contents are a distillation of the thousands of hours and hundreds of thousands of pounds that have gone into the research and development of LDL's current product range.

The skills and techniques described have been hammered out in session after session of course autopsies. Our professional preoccupation since 1974 has been to forge, at least to our own satisfaction, a basic grammar of salesmanship which is effective in today's market place.

Read it, study it, apply it. A single, simple idea received and then deliberately practised could repay your investment a hundred times over.

I hope you enjoy it.

Robin Fielder

Are you a professional?

You hear of the professional accountant, solicitor, architect, engineer, doctor, but you can have a professional *anything*.

The word 'professional' does not go with the occupation, it goes with the person.

It describes a method of doing something.
It implies a dedication to excellence.
It is intimately involved with your image.
It means integrity, that's what you would do even if you knew you wouldn't be found out.

A short course in human relations

the SIX most important words
"I ADMIT I MADE A MISTAKE"

the FIVE most important words
"YOU DID A GOOD JOB"

the FOUR most important words
"WHAT IS YOUR OPINION"

the THREE most important words
"WOULD YOU MIND"

the TWO most important words
"THANK YOU"

the one LEAST important word
"I"

Objections

Recent research into this subject has identified three key principles.

1. Don't enshrine objection handling.

Over the years the prominence given to objection handling skills both in books and sales training programmes suggests that they are crucial to effective selling.

Many salespeople regard objection handling as 'all powerful' — if only they had better answers to objections their results would really improve. One or two companies even have objection handling advisors, whose full time job is to come up with model answers to objections. This emphasis is misplaced. It doesn't matter how brilliantly an objection is answered, it has still created a gap between buyer and seller at the end of the presentation.

The emphasis should be on pre-handling. Obvious objections which almost always come up must be handled early on in the presentation.

2. The majority of objections are not inherent to the Buyer, but are created by the behaviour of the Seller.

Common sense suggests that for every hour of face to face selling time, two people selling the same products in a comparable market place would receive about the same number of objections. Research, however, indicates that this is not the case. In some sales teams one seller frequently had to handle 5 times as many objections as another, ie Inept selling advice creates objections.

Eg: Consider a computer systems salesperson making a 6 monthly follow-up call to a customer.

Seller: "Are you completely satisfied with the system?"

Buyer: "Not entirely the printer is a little slow."

Seller: (Seeing the opportunity to sell a faster printer) "Then what you need is our new high speed printer. It's 35% faster than the one you are currently using."

Buyer: "Yes, but it's not worth paying all that extra just for an increase in speed."

The PRICE objection!

What has happened is the seller has offered his solution, a faster printer, too soon. Many salespeople make this error, they offer their solution too early.

Salespeople who hold back on offering their solutions, until they have built a strong desire, not only receive fewer objections — they close more sales.

So to avoid the price objection show the prospect what it will save/make in pound terms FIRST. Build his judgement of value BEFORE offering the solution.

3. Know how to handle objections if and when they crop up.

Having discussed the importance of keeping the emphasis on pre-handling, it is nevertheless inevitable that objections are going to crop up from time to time and we must be able to handle them.

Every product or service has perhaps half a dozen objections, areas of mismatch, which customers often raise. It is essential to know how to handle these.

NB: New salespeople often fear objections. There is, therefore, considerable value in training them how to handle all the different objections which can occur. The danger point comes when the demand for training is objection handling, gives it more prominence than objection prevention.

Summary: Poor selling creates objections — the solution is not to become better at handling those objections, but to improve the presentation so they do not occur.

The objection handling material in this pocket course is divided into two parts:

Part I: How to pre-handle objections.

Part II: How to answer objections.

Part I — Pre-handling.

Consider this dialogue:

John's lawnmower packs up one Sunday afternoon, so he goes around to his neighbour to ask if he can borrow his.

John: "Can I borrow your lawnmower?"

Neighbour: "Sorry John, not today."

John: "Why not?"

Neighbour: "Because my mother is ill."

John: "Well, I'm sorry to hear that, but what has that got to do with my borrowing your lawnmower?"

Neighbour: "Absolutely nothing, but since I have decided not to lend it, one excuse is as good as another"

From this example we see that there are two types of objections:

(i) **Excuses** not to go ahead.

(ii) **Real objections, areas of mismatch.**

(Mismatch is a better description as the objection may simply be a misunderstanding, or a request for more information.)

When an objection occurs at the end of presentation we often don't know which type it is. This is why pre-handling is such an important skill.

IF IT'S AN EXCUSE, by pre-handling it — the prospect cannot then use it at the end.

eg: We know someone is short staffed and we want them to do something urgently — the obvious EOS (End of sale) excuse is "I'm short staffed."

We can pre-handle this by saying:

"I realise John is away at present and you're really pushed, but I would very much appreciate it if....."

He can't then use the EXCUSE "I'm short staffed."

OR IF IT'S A REAL OBJECTION and we discover it early on, we know where we stand and what we have to solve.

Early in the presentation we should pre-handle the objections we are likely to meet later on.

Note: Only pre-handle the obvious ones, otherwise we are making things unnecessarily more difficult.

eg **Delivery:** Everybody always leaves everything to the last minute. So delivery time is not the important parameter it's "When do you want it."
OR
"If you decided to go ahead, when would you want it installed and working."
This also pre-handles the EOS excuse "I won't need it for a few months yet."

Specification: "What are you looking for."
Pre-handles the EOS objection
"It's not quite what I'm looking for."

Refer to Board: "Are you able to make this decision alone or must you put it before the Board."
This pre-handles the EOS objection
"I must put it before the Board."

Rumours: The possibility of rumours affecting his decision should also be pre-handled

"Have you heard of product before."
"What do you know about us."
"Do you know any companies using..."
If rumour is bad, something to the detriment of product/service — must be pre-handled.

Price: People buy VALUE TO THEM. Pre-handle the EOS price objection by building the prospect's JUDGEMENT OF VALUE early in the presentation.
The higher we can build his opinion of the value and importance of his requirements early in the presentation, the easier it is for him to accept price later on.

Note: Show EXTRA price as more than compensated, not by extra benefits, but by extra MATCHING benefits.

Perhaps the biggest mistake salesmen make is trying to MATCH PRICE instead of SELLING SUPERIORITY.

Part II — Answering objections.

3. stage sequence:

Stage 1. Ask it back (Listen to it first!)

When the prospect brings up an objection it is usually an apple — the real objection, if it exists, is the core. So we must take bites out of the apple to see how close to the core we can get.

eg: "Price too high" could mean any of the following:

(i) More expensive than I thought
(ii) Outside budget
(iii) More than I can sanction
(iv) My job to reduce price
(v) Somebody else is cheaper
(vi) I have not got any money
(vii) I'm not convinced of the value
(viii) I want a discount
(ix) I'm not the decision maker
(x) I don't want the product/service

We must find out which in order to be able to handle it.

Examples of ASK BACK questions, that take another bite:

a) In relation to what
b) What exactly do you mean by that
c) Just to clarify my thinking, why is that important at this time
d) I'm sure you have a very good reason for saying that, do you mind if I ask you what it is
(see later in this booklet)

(Note, in certain cases, in trying to re-explain it to us he answers it himself — ie: there was no core).

Stage 2. Agree.

People buy people first — so agree with his view point.

This: 1) Softens objection in his mind
2) Avoids confrontation

Types of agreement:

Not: "Oh yes, I agree we are too expensive"
Not: "Yes but"

Instead:
(i) I can understand that
(ii) I can appreciate why you think that
(iii) That's a very good point, I'm glad you brought it up
(iv) I used to think the same myself
(v) That is exactly the initial reaction of many of our best customers
(vi) Perhaps I didn't explain that point fully

Stage 3. Answer.

3 approaches:

1. OUTWEIGH IT — by showing how advantages OUTWEIGH disadvantages.

Occasionally it is appropriate to use:
"I appreciate what you are faced with Mr Prospect, can I suggest something to clarify the situation. Let's take a sheet of paper, draw a line down the middle. On one side list all the advantages to you of using our services and on the other all the disadvantages."
List the advantages on the left hand side, the disadvantages on the right.

2. REMOVE IT — by showing it's not important IN HIS CASE.

3. WEAKEN IT — by showing IN PRACTICE it's not such a serious problem.

Examples — **Price objection:**

1. Ask back — "In relation to what"
Show value to him.

2. Reduce it to the smallest possible amount — the 'funny money' approach.

3. "I can buy cheaper elsewhere"
— "I'm sure you can, let me ask you — how much cheaper."
Show DIFFERENCE more than compensated for by extra MATCHING value.

4. "WHAT!"
Prospects will deliberately test us regarding price. Their objective is to lower our expectations, to lower our aspiration level. They are trained to do this, so don't be put off.

Competition and the price objection:

Buyer: "You are more expensive than....."

Seller: "That's correct but let me ask you, isn't it true that all companies have a choice to make. They can either provide a service which does as much as possible for their customers OR they can provide a service which does just enough for them to get by with. Isn't that the choice that every company must make?"

Buyer: "Yes"

Seller: "What would you like us to do for you, as much as possible or just enough to get by with"

Then remind buyer of matching benefits and remember to add value of 'you'
"You can't buy anything from my Company without getting me with it"

Credibility — 'How do I know'.

"We've never done business with you before, HOW DO I KNOW you will do what you say."

OR

HOW DO I KNOW whether or not there are other companies who offer a similar service but at less cost.

Solution, bring on your evidence.
eg: Selling to Managing Director

Seller: "If we had one or a number of other Managing Director's here with us today in this room, who were using these services, may I assume you would be guided by them."

Buyer: "Yes"

Seller: "Well they're not here, but this is what they have written."

Then bring on your evidence, testimonial letters and so forth.

"If we had one or a number of the Country's leading authorities on financial management here with us today in this room may I assume you would be guided by them."

"If we had one or a number of the Country's leading authorities on computer software here with us today in this room may I assume you would be guided by them.

"Just supposing you were convinced.... What would you do?"

This is a powerful phrase to overcome objections and get back in the sale.

IMPORTANT: This phrase is NOT suitable for opening the sale or for final closing — it is an objection handling phrase only.

The phrase may be used with or without "YOU WERE CONVINCED" or "YOU WERE CERTAIN IN YOUR MIND."

When we use the full phrase in many cases he tells us what he would do (He'd go ahead) then says "Convince me first." We then say "What would we have to do in order for you to be convinced?"

Applications — "I'm happy with my current supplier."

"JUST SUPPOSING YOU WERE CONVINCED there was another supplier who could do better and less expensively all the things you require — WHAT WOULD YOU DO?

"I'm satisfied with what I have now."

"JUST SUPPOSING YOU WERE CONVINCED there was a better product available, WHAT WOULD YOU DO?" OR "You'd want to find out more about it wouldn't you?"

"These things don't work."

"JUST SUPPOSING YOU WERE CONVINCED one did WHAT WOULD YOU DO?"

"These things are more trouble than they are worth."

"JUST SUPPOSING YOU WERE CONVINCED one was worth it, WHAT WOULD YOU DO?"

We can also use JUST SUPPOSING as an introduction to "Second supplier" techniques:

"JUST SUPPOSING your present supplier for some reason, could not maintain supplies — WHAT WOULD HAPPEN?
How long would it take you to get another supplier organised. Could you do it in the time?
SURELY it would be much more SATISFACTORY to have two suppliers — then if anything happened to one of them, you could easily increase business with the other."

Budgets

Firstly, understand what budgets are — they are bits of paper designed to ensure a balanced approach. They are not intended as restraints on making profits.

Objection: "I've got no budget."
OR "My budget is insufficient."

1. Talking to person who sets budget:

"JUST SUPPOSING YOU WERE CONVINCED that this would increase your profit by X WHAT WOULD YOU DO?"

Answer: "I'd buy it. I'd change the budget."

2. Talking to person who is given budget and who is himself convinced:

Prospect: "It's outside my budget."

Salesman: "Who sets the budget?"

Prospect: "The Board."

Salesman: "JUST SUPPOSING THEY WERE CONVINCED that by doing this they would achieve savings of Y WHAT WOULD THEY DO?"

Prospect: "They would go ahead."

Salesman: "So what WE'VE got to do is get to the Board — Can you fix it up?"

OR: "JUST SUPPOSING the people who set the budgets realised this would save £Y,000 WHAT WOULD THEY DO?"

"Don't you think they would like to know about it?"

"I'm sure you have a very good reason for saying that, do you mind if I ask you what it is?"

This phrase is used whenever the prospect makes an "I'm not interested" or "I'm not interested in that" statement.

It replaces "WHY NOT" — don't use this, it's a high-pressure selling cliche and Prospects have built up a mental wall against it!

The object is to get to the bottom of the Prospect's "not interested." You must find out what is on his mind.

Examples:

> "I'm not interested in updating my equipment."
>
> "I'm sure you have a very good reason for saying that, do you mind if I ask you what it is?"
>
> "I have a closed mind on the subject."
>
> "I'm sure you have a very good reason for saying that, do you mind if I ask you what it is?"

Psychology of a sales process

The objective of any sales presentation is to get the prospect to 'act' to go ahead.

Action is only ever the result of motivation. Consequently any sales process should obey the laws of motivation. Be careful not to confuse with manipulation.

Motivation — getting people to do what THEY want to do.

Manipulation — getting people to do what WE want them to do.

No one is interested in what WE want, they are interested in what THEY want.

So, the two steps in a motivational, action producing presentation are:

> Step 1: find out what they want, and then
>
> Step 2: show them how to get it.

This can be re-defined as:

The successful presentation involves:—

> (i) FINDING what the Prospect wants, and then
>
> (ii) MATCHING our product/service to it.

Sell matching benefits

In basic sales training sales people are taught the importance of converting features into benefits. Converting what it IS into what it will DO for the prospect.

eg: This overhead projector has a Xenon gas lamp (feature) which means that light output is very high and people sitting at the back of a large hall can still see clearly (benefit).

This basic skill is obviously vital. However, research indicates that the concept of selling benefits, which for years has been the key to effective selling is incomplete.

The subject of selling skills like most other disciplines has progressed.

The modern approach is to sell MATCHING benefits.

What makes product 'A' superior to product 'B' is NOT the fact that it has more features and consequently more benefits, BUT THAT IT DOES MORE OF WHAT THE PROSPECT WANTS IT TO DO. ie. It has more matching benefits.

Sell matching benefits.

Anti-aircraft systems

Consider a parallel between a world war II anti-aircraft installation and a modern surface to air heat seeking missile.

The old pom-pom guns turned the air black with air burst explosive but you saw very few hits. A large amount of energy was expended in the general direction of the target without much accuracy.
This is similar to the traditional 'canned' presentation of the so called 'representative', all the features and all the benefits are aimed in the general direction of the sale.
This is inaccurate and consequently difficult to close.

The heat seeking missile has a sensor which detects heat produced by the enemy aircraft. This feedback enables the missile to continually adjust its trajectory. The result is greatly improved accuracy.

The same principle applies to professional selling. We must continually ask questions throughout the presentation. This produces feedback — what the prospect wants — which enables us to adjust the presentation and ensure accurate matching.

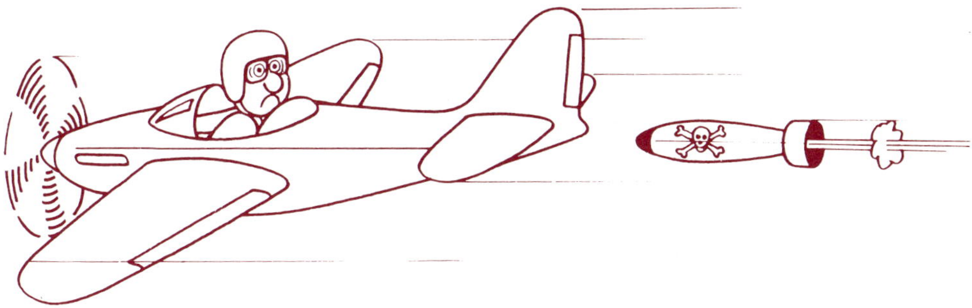

Closing questions

Ask for the order and get it.

Ever since man began selling, a sales manager's greatest tribute has been, "He's a good closer." And every sales manager's most common complaint has been, "He makes a good presentation, but he doesn't know how to close."

Many sales training programmes are very comprehensive until they get to closing. They give it a once over light treatment, avoiding it as the most difficult part of selling. Some, regretably, have surrounded it with a psychic aura, a mysticism that has been more confusing than helpful.

Closing is straightforward — You close business by asking for it.

Important points:

Always ask a closing question, don't HINT at a close.

Questions demand answers.
Don't make the error of finishing with a closing STATEMENT.

Prospects EXPECT a good salesperson to ask for the order at the end of the presentation. So don't disappoint them!

If you don't ask for the order, you're working for the competition.

Never let a sale you've worked for go unasked for.

Don't mistake hesitance for refusal — it's natural for people to hesitate before making a decision.

Shut up and wait for the answer after your closing question!

When to close

The object of a sales presentation is to find out what the prospect wants and then match to it. Once this is achieved we then ask for the order. However, if we ask for the order BEFORE the matching is complete we will get objections. So, we must be careful not to close too early. The correct time to ask a closing question is when the matching is complete. Consequently, prior to closing, we should test the matching by asking a TEST CLOSE question.

Examples: How do you feel about that?
How does that strike you?
Are you happy with everything?
Do you have a date in mind?
Do you have any other questions about it?

If we get a positive answer — then close, ask for the order.

If we get a negative answer — do not close. Find out what he is unsure of.

Techniques (all are used after the Test Close).
You close business by asking for it, and you usually ask for it in one of three ways:

1. The alternative close.

This is the easiest form of closing questions and so it should be used as often as possible. We give the prospect a choice between two alternatives — a choice of delivery date, financial arrangements, quantity, colour etc. The choice should be of a minor nature and both alternatives should be attractive to the prospect. His answer reflects his personal preference. When he answers he has committed himself to order.

"Would you like delivery this month or next?"

"Would you prefer to invest in this outright or make use of our leasing arrangements?"

"This item comes in two colours green and red, they are both popular, which one would you prefer?"

The alternative close.

2. The direct close.

This is a straightforward request for the business.

It is uncomplicated and reflects the salesperson's confidence in the presentation.
Once again it must be used after a Test Close.

Examples:

"Are you happy with everything?" (Test close)
"Can we go ahead and get the order moving?"

"Do you have any other questions about it?" (Test close)
"Good, then if you are satisfied can I write up the order?"

Other examples:

"Shall I put you down for 10 terminals?"

"Can I have your OK to start delivery next week?"

"Can we install it for you right away?"

"Can we call it a deal?"

"How about it, can we go ahead right away?"

"Will you give us your approval to go ahead?"

"Can we have your order?"

3. The step by step close.

For large sales.

Use this when the prospect finds it difficult to make major decisions.

We seek his agreement to our proposal one step at a time, usually with a series of alternative closing questions on minor aspects of the sale.

By successively gaining his agreement to minor points we finish up with agreement on the major decision.

Success by the inch is a cinch, by the yard it is hard.

Beating your competition

Six Principles:

1. Wherever possible, don't talk about your competitors at all.

Just because you are in a competitive market, don't always assume you are up against competition. You might be or you might not be.

Business is often lost because the seller is too aware of the competition and consequently inadvertently suggests it to his prospect with the phrase:
'Are you seeing anybody else.' This is the classic error. Never use this phrase as the prospect thinks – maybe I should!

Are you seeing anybody else?

Instead, in order to test whether or not we are up against competition ask:
'Have you done anything about this so far?"
OR
"How far have you got with this?"
OR
"What plans have you got for solving this situation?"

2. If you must talk about them:

Don't call them 'Our competitors'
Don't say 'The Competition'
Don't say 'Compare us with'

All these phrases simply add credibility to the strength of your so called competition.

Instead call them:

'Other companies'
'Other manufacturers'

If someone says to you "Who are your competitors?"

Be positive, answer, "I don't know, we haven't got any, there are a number of other companies in the same business as us. There are even some who have products with a similar name, but that's where the similarity ends because of........"

And then accentuate the DIFFERENCE, sell the difference.

3. Don't knock your competitors.

Knocking is unprofessional, it's amateurish and most people regard it as such. It also breaks the basic rule of business – what you hand out, you get back.

HE KNOWS you think your product/service is better, HE WANTS TO KNOW WHY.

If you must talk about them it is better to praise them.

– "They are good at many things, but we are better, here's why."

But don't get too carried away with praise, remember the rule – Pay the highest compliment to the least likely contender!

Praise will also work well against competition should they choose to speak badly of you.

In this context, remember the system/product he already has is in competition with your product. The NO KNOCKING rule still applies. The customer may not like what he has but deep down he still believes he made a right decision. This means, don't join in with him if he starts complaining about what he has. Instead say "I know what you mean, however when you chose......it was the best on the market, now there is something better and that is why I am here."

Note: No knocking does not necessarily mean don't point out their weaknesses or drawbacks. It means don't say nasty, unpleasant things about them. Don't criticise their products, services or staff. Don't condemn what they do.

4. **What they do well, everyone does well – including us.** Then accentuate the difference, eg:

   "To be quite fair Mr Prospect, today all TV sets have an outstanding picture quality, but we believe in XYZ TV that having this additional facility is vital and we are the only Company that provides this."

5. **Wherever possible, never mention your competitors by name.**
   It's free advertising.
   It raises prospect's confidence in your competition.
   Instead, as mentioned earlier, call them 'other' companies, 'other' manufacturers.

6. Establish your Unique Sales Points (USP).

Selling against competition is all about selling the difference. First, you must establish what this difference is – what are your unique sales points. What can you offer that other suppliers cannot.

Sit down for a few hours with a number of your colleagues and ask these questions: –

> Why do people buy from us?
> List down all the reasons your group comes up with.

Then ask:

> Why do people buy from our so-called competitors?
> Get all the reasons down.

This will enable you to identify what the differences are.

Then call your best five customers and ask them why they bought from your Company. Their reasons are often different to those we were expecting.

Differences usually occur in three areas:

i) Product or service differences,
ii) Company differences – locations, policy, transport,
iii) You – ask yourself: "What can I do that my competitors salespeople are unlikely to do?"

The difference is what takes you out of competition. The difference enables you to build belief in the sales team that you have no competition.

Having established the difference, then think about the benefits these unique sales points give to your prospective customers.

Then build desire for the difference by matching these USP benefits to what the prospect wants.

Ten important principles

The first sale we have to make is to ourselves.

1. Believe in what you're offering.

Consider this article written by an advertising executive:

"If there was ever a man who used belief in himself to tremendous advantage it was Mr X. He came to this department as a young man and learned the coffee roasting and blending business. He concluded that he could do better if he were in business for himself. HE THOROUGHLY BELIEVED that he could blend the best coffee, and even up to the time of his retirement, after years in the business; he thoroughly believed that his coffee was the best on the market. Of course, that belief made a millionaire of the man."

When we BELIEVE in what we're offering it comes across to the prospect and it's very persuasive.

Remember, the first sale we have to make is to ourselves. If we are convinced, we will be able to convince others and vice-versea.

2. Be a good listener.

We have two ears and one mouth. We should use them in that proportion.

A good conversationalist is a good listener.

A good salesperson is a good listener.

By listening we obtain more raw material on which to base sound judgements. In business, above average people monopolise the listening, below average people monopolise the talking.

Think about this amusing description:

People who talk about other people are gossips,
People who talk about themselves are boring,
People who talk about me are brilliant conversationalists.

So check your conversation!

3. Forget the tell, develop the ask.

Many salespeople make the mistake of just making statements. Instead we should make statements which end in a question.

In business if we keep asking questions, people keep answering them.

There are two types of questions:

Open questions: These are questions that cannot be answered with a simple 'yes' or 'no'. They are designed to obtain information by a descriptive response and begin with: –
WHO? WHAT? WHEN? WHERE? HOW? IF?

Some examples are: –
What are you looking for?
Where do you feel your current system could be improved?
What would a company have to offer in order to do business with you?
What specifically do you want to achieve?

Closed questions: Closed questions are those to which the answer is 'yes' or 'no'. They are used to confirm and control the conversation.
These questions usually start with: –
DO YOU? WOULD YOU? COULD YOU? ARE YOU? HAVE YOU?

When we 'close' a sales presentation we require a 'yes' answer consequently all questions that ask for the order are of the 'closed' type.

4. Don't talk down to people.

'I expect you are aware' is better than 'you're probably not aware'.

5. Selling is not a contest where one wins and one loses. Either both win or both lose.

The concept is WIN – WIN.

If you have a problem and we help you solve it, you're better off; and when you solve it with one of our products/services, we're both better off.
The fact is the only sale which is a good one is when we're BOTH better off.
The concept is WIN – WIN, we both have to win.

You see a top salesman, he's a winner, but how you measure his winnings is by how many other people won as a result of his service.

Make sure your belief in this concept comes across.

6. Vary your voice: –

Change rate of speaking,
Change volume of speaking,
Use silence.

7. Develop an empathy/ego balance.

Empathy: – the ability to put ourselves in the prospect's shoes – to thoroughly understand the prospect's problem and see the solution.

Ego: – Ego Drive (not to be confused with conceit or big-headedness – that's 'ego problem'!)
– the will to win.

Let's examine what happens when not in balance.

Strong empathy, weak ego drive:
We think he does well but he doesn't.
Prospects like him but usually end up buying from someone else.
He lacks the drive to finally convince people. He is a bad closer.

Strong ego drive, weak empathy:

He'll achieve some success, but failing to understand his prospect's problems he convinces few.

Balance is the key – Strong empathy AND strong ego drive.

8. Avoid procrastination by training yourself to act in response to do it now!

People who procrastinate miss things, they may be late for an appointment, they may miss a train, but more importantly they may miss an opportunity that could change their lives for the better.

You may recall the story of the Babylonian merchant and his camel. They both travelled with a wealthy caravan. One night the temperature dropped, it became cold and the camel begged to warm his nose – only his nose – in the merchant's tent.

You can guess what happened. Little by little the camel inched in his head, his shoulders, his front legs, first one hump and then the other until finally he took over the entire tent. The merchant was out in the cold.

This is exactly the same way in which procrastination can inch its way into our lives. Every time we procrastinate or put off until tomorrow what we can today, it creeps up on us – it takes over a larger part of our life.

Three familiar words are required DO IT NOW!

Getting more things done, becoming an action person who makes use of every opportunity does not require the memorisation of some complex psychological system, it simply requires relentless determination to ACT in response to DO IT NOW! and to keep this up over a long enough period of time to make it a habit – an automatic reflex.

Perhaps the most overlooked application of DO IT NOW! is in relation to our own ideas. We all have a certain timidity towards ideas we think of – Ideas are personal things, part of the person who gives them birth. Most of us treat criticism of our ideas in the same way we treat criticism of ourselves. Those of us who might otherwise be creative tend to remain silent for fear of this criticism. DO IT NOW! gets us into action before we have time to think about possible criticism.

9. Make each hour count.

If we make each hour count, then each day, each week, each month counts.

An hour in our career is like a single brick in the building of a house. A house consists of thousands of bricks but each one carries part of the load and makes up part of the appearance of the finished structure. If we make each hour count, we will build an outstanding career.

Have the phrase: 'What am I doing NOW to get a sale' on a card where you will see it often.

10. Convert excess tension relieving time into goal achieving time.

Consider how the hours during the day are broken down. They fall into two distinct areas of activity. The first is goal achieving, the second is tension relieving. Goal achieving is the time we spend progressively moving towards our goal, moving through the particular stages of our plan. Tension relieving is the relaxation, the unwinding that each of us needs every day, but we only need so much of this unwinding to recover from the stress and strain of daily life. Any excess is waste – and if we want to be a success, it is this 'excess' which we must transfer into goal achieving time.

Negotiating tactics

The difference between selling and negotiating

The process of salesmanship is to raise the prospect's perception of the value of your products/services to the point where he want to purchase.

Having decided to go ahead the prospect then turns his attention to the terms and conditions of the sale.

He now seeks a better deal in such areas as: discount, credit, specification, delivery.

The give and take process surrounding the terms and conditions of the sale is what negotiation is about.

For many buyers considerable job satisfaction comes from 'playing the game well' so the seller must be equipped to handle this area.

Negotiation is all about movement towards a mutually acceptable agreement – WIN – WIN.

18 Important points

1. Buyers in many instances will deliberately attempt to lower the seller's aspirations. They want to pull the seller out of position.

   This is done by: Showing surprise at the price.
Talking about competitors quotations.
Explaining budget restrictions.

   In many cases (but not all) it's a professional ploy, so don't be put off!

2. Don't give concessions, TRADE them.

   If you give a concession, don't just give it away, trade it for one from the buyer.

   Eg: If the concession is a discount, trade it for prompt payment or different delivery arrangements or a larger order.

3. Concessions can be 'actual' or 'apparent'.

4. The best concession is one which is cheap to you, but valuable to the buyer. That way you both WIN.

5. When you give a concession, raise the apparent COST to you.

   The concession will not be rated highly by the buyer unless we raise the apparent cost to us.

   Make a small move on your part seem large to him.

6. Raise the VALUE of your concession to him, by stressing the benefit it provides.

7. Minimise the value to you of his concession – aloud!

8. Remember you both have to continue working together after the deal has been struck, so don't leave him feeling he's lost, leave him thinking he's made a good deal.

   A good negotiator is very aware of allowing people to save face.

9. Concessions should be traded carefully. Don't take your hands off them until the buyer has agreed what he is going to do in return.

10. Explore concessions and negotiable areas with the phrase:

    IF you agree to do.....THEN we will.....

11. Don't dig your heels in too early. This produces stalemate. Be willing to move. Somewhere between everything you want and everything he wants you are bound to find an agreement that satisfies you both.

12. If deadlocked, point out the time investment and suggest another look through all the aspects before admitting defeat.

13. Don't give concessions too easily. Trade them reluctantly and one by one.

    Attempt to persuade the buyer that the benefits of the deal without the concession still justify acceptance.

14. Whenever you are ready to say 'yes' to a deal, practise saying 'NO' a few more times.

15. Watch your concession behaviour just before deadlines. Research indicates people make their biggest concessions just before deadlines.

    So, when you get close to a deadline, ask yourself, "What's wrong with half the amount I was thinking about?"

16. Always find out the buyers workload. If it's heavy, he will tend to settle more quickly.

17. If the buyer has several points he wants to negotiate get ALL of them before starting.

    Keep the whole deal in mind as you negotiate, perhaps you can offer him a concession in one area in return for something you want in another.

    Be careful of phrases like: "One final point and we're in business", "It would be fairer to both of us", "We're agreed apart from a few minor details".

18. Prepare thoroughly. Know all the negotiable variables you have at your disposal and keep searching for more.

Making appointments by telephone

Get through to the decision maker.

The objective is to sell the appointment, not your product or service.

Before making the call

Decide who to contact, determine the buying authority.
The 'buyer' is not necessarily the decision maker.

Ask yourself:	"What job function will benefit most from my product of service?"
Aim high:	Aim to speak to the most senior person. It is preferable to begin speaking to the Sales Director and be passed down by him to the Sales Manager, than to speak to the Sales Manager and be told that the responsibility for such things lies with the Sales Director.
Ask the switchboard:	"Who is in charge of, or, responsible for say, computer software?"

Establish the name of your prospect including his first name. Not Mr Smith but John Smith.

Getting through to the decision maker

Dial yourself, don't get someone else to do it. This avoids "I'm sorry he was here a minute ago."

Operator: "Bloggs Engineering"

Philips: "John Smith please" (Use first name, this sounds as if we know him.)

Operator: "Putting you through"

Secretary: "John Smith's office"

Philips: "IS HE IN?"

This phrase is invaluable as many secretaries screen sales people from their busy boss by saying he's not there.

Secretary: "Yes, but who is speaking?"
She can no longer say he's not there.

Philips: "David Philips from Go Fast Systems"

This may satisfy some secretaries who will put you through but usually she will ask:

Secretary: "What is it about?"

Answer with a benefit to her boss, in many instances if you make it sound complicated she will put you through just in case it's important.

Philips: "I want to talk to him about high efficiency computer software, he is still in charge of software isn't he?"

Secretary: "Yes"

Philips: "Great, can I speak to him please"

Usually this suffices, if it doesn't here are some ideas:

1. Make an ally of her. Ask for her help in the best way to present your case to him. This is always a good idea.

2. Persist.

   Call several times, say twice a week for a month. She will finally say to her boss "Oh you must call David Philips, he must have called eight times. I don't know what to say to him anymore, do have a word with him."

3. Call in her lunch hour.

4. Call before or after normal working hours – secretaries are not usually there but bosses often are.

5. Find out when she's on holiday! (If you don't your competitors will!)

When you get through the sequence is 6 fold: –

1. Check you are speaking to the right person. "Is that Mr Smith?"

2. Introduce yourself. Include your first name, don't call yourself Mr/Mrs/Miss but call him Mr.

   "Mr Smith my name is David Philips from Go Fast Systems."

3. Open the conversation with a relevant comment.

   "It's been a long time since we've been in contact".
   "I noticed you have just won a large export order".
   "We have a mutual friend in Frank Davis who suggested I contact you."

4. Now use your Opening Hot Button Statement (OHBS).

This is a general "What's in it for him' statement designed to spark his interest.

   "Mr Smith, we have been able to assist a number of other companies in a similar line to yourselves save up to 15% on their data retrieval costs. I have no idea whether or not this would be of a benefit to you so I'd like to come along and explain it to you."

5. Close on the appointment.

Rules: i) Offer a choice of two times. That way he is thinking 'when' to see us and not 'whether' to see us.

ii) Avoid 11.00am and 3.00pm. All salespeople ask for those, so this is when competition for his time is fierce.

iii) Unusual times – not on the hour or half-hour – suggest it will not take long, therefore he is more likely to want to see us.

eg: "Would it be more convenient to see you at 10.20 on Tuesday morning or sometime on Friday afternoon." (Don't make both alternatives unusual times that's going over the top!)

6. Repeat the arrangement.

"Fine, Mr Smith I'll look forward to seeing you at 10.20 on Tuesday 14 March."

Objections

"Put literature in the post."

Eg: "Great, I will do that today, you will have it tomorrow. There are however, certain things I want to SHOW you. Therefore I would like to come and see you after you have had a chance to read the brochure."

OR: "The brochure only gives a little bit of information and we find that most of our customers have very special requirements and it's these I'd like to discuss with you."

"Will it take long?"
(This is not an objection.)

"About ten minutes unless you have some questions you want to ask me"

Ten attitude builders

Winning isn't the important thing.
It's everything!

1. Be a Winner, not a Loser.

Ten differences between a winner and a loser.

1) A winner makes mistakes and says "I was wrong". A loser says "It wasn't my fault".

2) A winner credits his good luck for winning even though it wasn't luck. A loser credits his bad luck for losing, but it wasn't luck.

3) A winner works harder than a loser and has more time. A loser is always "too busy", too busy staying a failure.

4) A winner goes through a problem and a loser goes around it.

5) A winner shows he's sorry by making up for it. A loser says he's sorry but he does the same thing next time.

Be a Winner, not a Loser.

6) A winner knows what to fight for and what to compromise on. A loser compromises on what he should not and fights for what isn't worth fighting for. Every day is a battle of life and it is very important that we are fighting for the right things and not wasting our time with trivia.

7) A winner says "I'm good, but not as good as I ought to be". A loser says "Well, I'm not as bad as a lot of other people". A winner looks up to where he is going. A loser looks down at those who've not yet achieved the position he has.

8) A winner respects those who are superior to him and tries to learn from them. A loser resents those who are superior to him and tries to find fault.

9) A winner is responsible for more than his job. A loser says "I only work here".

10) A winner says "There ought to be a better way of doing it". A loser says "Why change it – that's the way it's always been done".

2. Stop rationalising away sales failure

Two dimensional sales people improve:
Product knowledge
Sales skills

Three dimensional salespeople improve:
Product knowledge
Sales skills
and THEMSELVES

The 3rd Dimension is our personality, charisma, drive, confidence, projection, persuasion and attitude.

TWO dimensional salesmen make the mistake of rationalising away sales failures.

They blame their lack of success on such things as:—

1. Product/service does not have all the features it should
2. Our price is too high
3. Range is too limited
4. Advertising no good
5. I went at the wrong time
6. The Recession
7. I've got a poor area
8. Prospect incapable of acting in his own best interest
9. Product quality too low
10. Competition is too good

This is natural — no-one likes to admit the mistake was theirs.

The THREE dimensional salesman does the following:—

1. He has a willingness to accept that selling failures are generally attributable to himself
2. He has the courage to dig out his mistakes
3. He makes up his mind not to repeat them

He ANALYSES each sales failure — he asks himself:

For example

1. Did I fail to gain Prospect's attention at the start?
2. Did I annoy Prospect with my mannerisms?
3. Did I arrive thinking negatively?
4. At what point did I lose the Prospect?
5. Did I try to be too nice?
6. Did I really find out what the Prospect wanted?
7. Did I match correctly?
8. Did I mention features without stressing benefits?
9. Did I get too technical?
10. Did I fail to answer a genuine question properly?
11. Did I get bogged down in handling objections?
12. Did I close too early?

Make your own list, it will be long to start with — then isolate them down to the 3 or 4 points which apply to you.

3. Be positive

Success comes in 'cans' not 'cannots.'

Consider a water jug with the level at the half way mark:
To the positive person it is ½ full;
To the negative person it is ½ empty.

Positive people see opportunity in adversity. Negative people think the grass is brown on both sides of the fence!

Think about these examples:

Eg: a) I've tried but people just don't want to buy — people just don't want it.

b) So far I've not been able to sell this product. But I know it's good and I'm going to keep at it until I find the formula.

To the Positive it's half full.
To the Negative it's half empty.

a) Competition has ALL the advantages — how do you expect me to sell against them.

b) Competition is strong that's true — but no one EVER has all the advantages — let's put our heads together and find a way to beat them.

a) The problem is too great, it's impossible to solve.

b) It's not a problem, it's a situation and a solution does exist — all we have to do is find it.

a) It's no use, we're beaten.

b) We're not beaten yet — let's keep trying — here's a new idea.

a) It won't work — let me prove it.

b) It will work — let me prove it.

a) The market is saturated — imagine 75% of the potential is already filled by other companies.

b) Imagine 25% of the market is wide open — let's get started — this looks exciting.

Life's battles don't always go

To the stronger or faster man,

But sooner or later the man who wins

Is the man WHO THINKS HE CAN.

4. Don't waste energy worrying and blaming

Worrying and blaming says "I'm not in charge."

A major cause of business failure is complaining instead of creating.

Cast your mind back to the Apollo 13 flight commanded by Jim Lovell. There was an explosion on board, immediately afterwards Lovell spoke to Houston and said a phrase which has become almost as famous as the Apollo flights themselves, he said:

"Houston, we have a problem," and everyone at Mission Control, on hearing that knew that Jim Lovell was in charge of Jim Lovell. What would you have said? How would you have reacted? There you are up there in a spacecraft built by the lowest bidder and part of it explodes!

The overwhelming natural tendency is to worry about it, to blame others, but Lovell and the hundreds of other people involved kept their minds focused on solving the situation, which they did.

We can all learn from this, we each have a certain amount of creative energy — we can either waste it worrying and blaming others or we can focus it on solving business set backs.

When things go wrong we should each ask ourselves:

Am I part of the problem
OR
Am I part of the solution

And finally, resist the temptation to tell others your problems — half of them don't care and the other half are glad!

5. Cultivate the habit of going the extra mile

Be willing to do more than is either expected or required.
Give extra service happily.
The person who does more than he is paid for, is soon willingly paid more.
Ask yourself: "How can I increase my service today?"
For a short time we may find we are worth more than we get, but the two will match up. They have to.

The average employee does just enough work not to get FIRED, and in return, the average employer pays just enough money to keep people from QUITTING and on that happy basis they go through life!

6. When in doubt — think what a failure would do and do the opposite

Success is unusual — achieved by the minority of people.

This means success is NOT to be achieved by:

1) Doing what everybody else does
2) Following our usual likes and dislikes — our usual habits!
3) Being guided by our natural preferences and prejudices
4) JUST doing what comes NATURALLY

The common-denominator of success, the one factor present in every success story is:

FORMING THE HABIT OF DOING WHAT FAILURES DON'T LIKE TO DO

eg: Setting goals, planning, working on ourselves, using time efficiently, avoiding frequent coffee breaks and long unproductive lunch hours, cutting down on unnecessary conversations in goal achieving time with people who are neither prospects nor customers.

The common-denominator of success can be used to overcome difficult business situations — Think what a failure would do in the same circumstances and DO THE OPPOSITE!

7. People buy people first and whatever else second

Consider this article written by the director of a Management Consultancy:

"My company had obtained a contract to provide consulting services to a relatively small bottling concern. The contract was substantial, amounting to £30,000. The client had little formal education. His business was in bad shape, and in recent years he had made some very costly mistakes.

Three days after we had got the contract, an associate and I were driving out to his plant. To this day I don't know how it started, but somehow we began talking about the negative qualities of our client.

Before we realised it, we were talking about how his own stupidity had brought about the mess he was in, instead of discussing how we could best approach solving his problems.

I remember one remark I made which I thought particularly clever — "The only thing holding up Mr X is fat!" My associate laughed and came up with an equally choice observation.

The whole drive out we talked about nothing else but what a weak idiot we had as a client.

Well, the meeting that afternoon was cold. Looking back, I think our client sensed somehow the way we felt towards him. He must have thought 'These people think I'm stupid and all they're going to do for my money is give me some high-sounding talk.'

Two days later I got a two-sentence letter from this client. It said, 'I've decided to cancel our contract for your consulting services. If there is a charge for your services to date, please invoice me.'

Priming ourselves with negative thoughts cost us a £30,000 contract. What made it even more painful was learning a month later that he had contracted with another consultancy for the same services.

We would never have lost him had we concentrated on his many fine qualities. And he has them. Most people do.

8. Decide to be outstanding

Have you ever thought about the thousands of people who say "I'm searching for myself" — who feel they have great potential but just don't know WHAT it is?

They read books on how to discover the 'self.' They go to vocational guidance searching for what will develop this potential.

But they never find it because nothing is there!

That's what people find when they search for the 'self' — nothing.

THE SELF ISN'T FOUND IT'S CREATED.

We don't discover our potential, we decide on it and then go to work developing it.

People become excellent by first deciding they are going to be excellent, then doing something about it.

So, to discover our greatest potential — the ONE thing we are really good at — here's what we do:—

DECIDE!

Decide WHAT we are going to be excellent at and then go to work developing it.

And we can get there faster by continuously asking ourselves:—

"If I were the top man in my business, how would I handle this."

9. Be a progressive thinker

Think progress. Believe in progress. Push for progress. Everything around us is growing. We can't stand still, we can either move forwards with it or drop back. It is impossible to be in business today, use yesterday's skills and expect to be in front tomorrow.

7 Ideas:

1) Don't let tradition — "Why change it, that's the way it's always been done" stagnate your mind. Instead experiment — try new approaches.

2) Become a "How can I do it better?" person. When you ask yourself this, your creative power is switched on. Remember the phrase: Good better best, never let it rest, until your good is better and your better is best!

3) Ask yourself "How can I do more?"
Capacity IS a state of mind.

4) Eliminate 'Impossible' 'Won't work' 'Can't do it' from both your speaking and thinking vocabulary when appraising new ideas.

5) Become an enthusiast for your profession. Thousands start a new job and wait for the job to prove itself to them. It never will, the job couldn't care less.
It's unimportant when we get into the business, what matters is when the business gets into us.

6) If you were an outside investor, would you invest in you?

7) S-T-R-E-T-C-H your mind. Associate with people who can help you think of new ideas, new ways of doing things. Mix with people of different social and business interests.

Remember, a mind that feeds only on itself, rapidly becomes undernourished and incapable of creative thought.

10. Don't ever quit

Quitters never win.
Winners never quit.
Making mistakes in business is inevitable. A man who says he has never made a mistake has never done anything. However, there is one mistake you must never make. Don't quit.

Don't Quit

When things go wrong, as they sometimes will,
When the road you're trudging seems all uphill,
When the funds are low and the debts are high,
And you want to smile, but you have to sigh,
When care is pressing you down a bit —
Rest if you must, but don't you quit.

Life is queer with its twists and turns,
As every one of us sometimes learns,
And many a fellow turns about
When he might have won had he stuck it out.
Don't give up though the pace seems slow —
You may succeed with another blow.

Often the goal is nearer than
It seems to a faint and faltering man;
Often the struggler has given up
When he might have captured the victor's cup;
And he learned too late when the night came down,
How close he was to the golden crown.

Success is failure turned inside out —
The silver tint of the clouds of doubt,
And you never can tell how close you are,
It may be near when it seems afar;
So stick to the fight when you're hardest hit —
It's when things seem worst that you mustn't quit.

...Anon